Greek Cuisine Cookbook

50 Easy and Delicious Greek Recipes

By

Patrick Smith

ISBN-10: 1500505714
ISBN-13: 978-1500505714

Contents

Section 1: Breakfast

1. Greek Yogurt Egg Pie

There is a lot more than eggs in this breakfast quiche. It has bacon, potatoes and yogurt, and is ready in only 20 minutes.

8 slices **turkey bacon**
1/3 cup yellow **onion** (thinly sliced)
3 **russet potatoes**
¼ cup non-fat **Greek yogurt**
½ tsp **salt** (ground)
¼ tsp **black pepper** (ground)
4 whole **eggs**
4 **egg whites**
1 tsp **Italian** seasoning

Makes 8 servings
Calorie: 122 per serving

Pierce potatoes and microwave for about 5 minutes. Remove and allow to cool, then peel and slice. Set aside.

In a skillet, brown turkey bacon and drain over paper towels. In the same pan, still containing the bacon grease, sauté onions until browned. Mix in potatoes and bacon.

Meanwhile, combine eggs and the rest of the ingredients in a bowl. Add the mixture to the skillet. Lower heat, cover and simmer for about 10 minutes.

Enjoy!

2. Greek Raspberry Breakfast

It only takes 15 minutes to jumpstart your day with this healthy yogurt, fruit and cereal breakfast.

1 ½ cups **raspberries**
3 oz. (85 g) crunchy **oat cereal**
2 ½ cups **Greek yogurt**

Makes 4 servings
Calorie: 24 per serving

Set a broiler to high heat. Evenly spread cereals on a baking sheet and broil for about 4 minutes. Remove and allow to cool.

In a bowl, mix yogurt with cooled cereals, then add 1 cup of raspberries. Scoop into serving glasses, topped with the remaining berries. Serve immediately.

Enjoy!

3. Pita Pocket Breakfast

A delicious combination of scrambled eggs, sausage, and Swiss cheese. It is ready in about 25 minutes.

5 slices **Swiss cheese** (halved)
1 lb. (450 g) bulk pork **sausage**
5 **pita breads** (halved)
½ tsp dried **oregano**
5 whole **eggs**
¼ cup **milk**
¼ tsp each **pepper** and **salt**

Makes 10 servings
Calories: 113 per serving

Preheat oven to 300°F (150°C) and prepare a baking pan.

In the pan, brown sausage over medium heat. Drain on paper towels and set aside.

Place the pita halves in the pan and toast for about 5 minutes.

In a bowl, whisk eggs with oregano and milk, then season with salt and pepper. Transfer to a lightly oiled pan and cook over medium heat, until eggs are done. Mix in the sausages.

Prepare pita halves by layering each with a slice of cheese and about 1/3 cup of egg mixture. Serve warm.

Enjoy!

4. Cheesy Herbed Eggs

The flavourful mix of herbs and cheese provides the eggs with a savoury taste. Total preparation time is 25 minutes.

16 whole **eggs** (beaten)
¼ cup **butter**
1 cup **half-and-half cream**
1 tsp **lemon peel** (grated)
¼ tsp dried **oregano**
¼ tsp dried **basil**
¼ tsp dried **rosemary** (crushed)
½ cup **parmesan** cheese (grated)
½ cup **cheddar** cheese (shredded)
1 tsp **salt**
½ tsp **pepper**
Tomato wedges (optional)

Makes 6-8 servings
Calories: 295 per serving

Combine lemon peel and cream in a mixing bowl. Beat in eggs and seasonings, then add the cheeses and mix well to blend.

In a large pan, heat butter until melted and add the egg mixture. Cook for about 15 minutes, stirring slowly over medium heat until eggs are cooked.

Serve with tomato wedges as garnish.

Enjoy!

5. Zucchini Feta Pancakes

This moist and tasty pancake is one best ways to use zucchini for breakfast. Total preparation time is about 30 minutes.

½ cup all-purpose **flour**
6 tsp **vegetable oil** (divided)
1 cup **feta cheese** (crumbled)
4 whole **eggs** (separated)
4 cups **zucchini** (shredded)
½ cup **green onions** (finely chopped)
1 tbs fresh **mint** (chopped)
½ tsp **salt**
¼ tsp **pepper**

Makes 4 servings
Calories: 257 per serving

In a bowl, whisk the egg whites until smooth. Set aside.

In a large bowl, whip the egg yolks with flour, feta cheese, onions, zucchini, mint, salt and pepper. Add the egg whites, fold to blend.

In a large pan, heat 2 teaspoons of oil over medium heat and fry 1/3 cupful of batter for about 2 minutes on each side, or until golden brown. Repeat for the rest of the batter.

Enjoy!

6. Greek Fruity Couscous

This couscous is too delicious to be just for side dishes. It makes a healthful breakfast in just 10 minutes.

2 ½ oz. (75 g) packet flaked **almonds**
1 cup clear **apple juice**
1 tbs **honey**
1/2 cup **sultanas**
2 green **apples** (grated)
2 freestone **peaches** (halved, chopped)
1 cup **couscous**

Makes 4 servings
Calories: 105 per serving

Preheat oven to 300 °F (180°C).

Combine honey and apple juice in a saucepan and bring to a boil. Remove from heat and set aside.

In bowl, combine couscous with the apple juice mixture. Mix to blend. Let sit for about 5 minutes for the grains to absorb the liquid.

Spread almonds on a baking sheet and bake for about 5 minutes. Remove and allow to cool

Add sultanas, peaches, apples and baked almonds to the couscous mixture. Mix to blend.

Top with a scoop of yoghurt.

Enjoy!

7. Minty Eggs with Turkish Bread

This is a delicious breakfast with eggs and Turkish bread. It takes 30 minutes to prepare.

1 ¼ cups **Greek yoghurt**
1/3 cup **olive oil** or **coconut oil**
1 large red **onion** (halved, sliced)
1 loaf **Turkish bread**, (halved horizontally)
½ cup **butter** (chopped)
6 whole **eggs**
1 clove **garlic** (crushed)
1 tsp ground **cumin**
2 **lemons** (juiced)
½ tsp dried **chilli** flakes
½ tsp **salt**
½ bunch **mint** (chopped)

Makes 5 servings
Calories: 166 per serving

Preheat oven to 390°F (200°C).
Arrange bread slices, cut-side up on a baking sheet. Sprinkle some oil and drizzle with salt and pepper to taste. Toast for 10 minutes.

While bread is toasting, heat remaining oil in a skillet over medium-low heat. Sauté onions, add salt and cook until tender. Stir in 2 tsp lemon juice, remove from heat and transfer to a bowl.

Clean the pan, then heat some butter and cook 2 eggs until whites are firm and yolks are runny. Gently transfer to a tray lined with parchment paper. Cook remaining eggs the same way.

On each slice of toasted bread, place 3 tbs yogurt and top with eggs and onions. Place the remaining butter in the pan and cook garlic and cumin for about 1 minute, stirring constantly.
Mix in remaining lemon juice, then season with salt. Cook for another minute.

Sprinkle butter mixture over eggs, then drizzle mint and chilli flakes on top. Slice each bread into desired serving sizes. Serve at once and enjoy!

8. Vegetable Frittata

This delicious breakfast is a bit more elaborate and rich in Mediterranean ingredients, containing lots of vegetables and various cheeses. It is prepared in about 1 hour.

¼ cup **Parmesan cheese** (shredded)
¼ cup **feta cheese** (crumbled)
1 cup **milk**
1 small **onion** (chopped)
1 medium **tomato** (sliced)
4 whole **eggs**
1 small yellow summer **squash** (sliced)
1 small **zucchini** (sliced)
1 garlic **clove** (minced)
1 cup **mozzarella cheese** (shredded)
2 tbs fresh **basil** (minced)
¼ tsp **pepper**
½ tsp **salt**

Makes 8 serving
Calories: 115 per serving

Preheat oven to 375°F (190°C). Lightly grease a pie plate.

Combine zucchini, squash, and onion in a heat-proof bowl. Cover and microwave on high setting for 8 minutes, or until tender. Drain and set aside.

Transfer to the prepared pie plate, then top with the feta cheese, mozzarella, and tomato slices.

Meanwhile, in a large bowl, beat the eggs with milk, basil, garlic, salt and pepper. Pour this over the tomato layer and sprinkle with Parmesan cheese.

Bake for about 45 minutes, or until a toothpick inserted comes out clean. Remove and allow to cool for 10-15 minutes.

Enjoy!

9. Greek Blueberry Breakfast

This recipe is very quick to prepare and contains few calories. It is perfect to balance out a recent overindulgence or if there is little time to make something more elaborate. It is ready in just 5 minutes.

¼ cup fresh **blueberries**
1 tsp **honey**
½ cup non-fat **Greek yogurt**
1 dash **cinnamon**
¼ cup **Walnuts**, **flaxseed**, or **almonds**

Makes 1 serving
Calorie: 37 per serving

Fill yogurt into a small serving bowl. Top with blueberries, drizzle honey, and sprinkle cinnamon.

Add almonds, walnuts, or flaxseeds (or mix all three).

Enjoy!

10. Greek Breakfast Burrito

Greek burritos are always an attraction, not only on the breakfast table but also at parties. They are fast, fun and easy to make.

2 whole **eggs**
1 ½ oz. (45 g) **cheddar cheese** (shredded)
2 tbs **salsa**
¼ **tomato** (diced)
¼ medium **onion** (diced)
¼ tbs **garlic** (minced)
¼ medium **bell pepper** (diced)
¼ tsp all-purpose **Greek seasoning**
2 flour **tortillas**
½ oz. (15 g) **cheddar cheese** (shredded)
2 oz. (55 g) **pepperoni**, (cubed)

Makes 2 servings
Calorie: 95 per serving

Preheat oven to 300°F (150°C)

Heat up a pan over medium-high heat. Add bell pepper, pepperoni, garlic, onion, tomato, and Greek seasoning, then cook for about 10 minutes. Stir in eggs and continue cooking until firm.

Spread egg mixture on the flour tortillas, then top with cheese and fold. Bake for about 10 minutes, or until cheese melts.

Remove from the oven and add salsa on top.

Enjoy!

Section 2: Lunch

1. Grilled Turkey Burgers

The taste of familiar Greek gyros is captured in these delicious creamy burgers. They take 20 minutes to prepare.

Yogurt Sauce
¼ cup red **onion** (chopped)
¼ cup **cucumber** (chopped)
½ cup low-fat **Greek yogurt**

Burgers
4 **burger buns** (split)
1 lb. lean **turkey** (ground)
½ tsp **garlic** powder
1 tsp dried **oregano** leaves
½ cup low-fat **Greek yogurt**
½ tsp **pepper**
½ tsp **salt**

Makes 4 burgers
Calories: 75 per serving

Preheat a grill on medium heat.

In a bowl, combine ingredients for the sauce. Chill until ready to serve.

In another bowl, combine ingredients for the burger. Shape into 4 patties, about ½ inch (1.3 cm) thick.

Place patties on grill, cover and grill for about 5 minutes on each side.

Serve patties in buns with the chilled sauce.

Enjoy!

2. Greek Penne Pasta Salad

Greek salad gets a twist in this recipe, combining cooked penne pasta with classic Mediterranean ingredients.

½ **cucumber** (sliced)
½ cup **black olives** (sliced)
2 cups **penne pasta**
1 tbs **lemon** juice
¼ cup **red wine vinegar**
2 cloves **garlic** (crushed)
2 tsp dried **oregano**
½ cup **feta cheese** (crumbled)
10 cherry **tomatoes** (halved)
2/3 cup **olive oil** (extra-virgin)
1 small **red onion** (chopped)
1 **red bell pepper** (chopped)
1 **green bell pepper** (chopped)
Salt and **pepper** to taste

Makes 8 servings
Calories: 55 per serving

Cook penne pasta according to package instructions until it is al dente. Drain in a colander and rinse with running water. Set aside.

For the sauce, whisk vinegar with garlic, oregano, lemon juice, olive oil, salt, and pepper in a bowl. Set aside.

In another large bowl, combine pasta with green and red peppers, tomatoes, onion, olives, cucumber, and feta cheese. Pour sauce over the pasta and toss to coat.

Either serve warm or cover and chill for another 3 hours before serving.

Enjoy!

3. Greek Chicken Stew

This slow-cooked chicken stew is a family favorite.

6 bone-in **chicken thighs** (skin removed)
2 cups baby-cut **carrots** (halved lengthwise)
1 tsp **cinnamon** (ground)
1 lb. (450 g) small whole **onions**
4 ½ oz. (400 g) **tomatoes** (diced, un-drained)
2 cloves **garlic** (finely chopped)
2 tsp **lemon peel** (grated)
1/3 cup **tomato paste**
¼ cup **parsley** (coarsely chopped)
½ tsp dried **oregano** leaves
½ tsp each **salt** and **pepper**

Makes 6 servings
Calories: 187 per serving

In a lightly greased slow cooker, place onions and carrots at the bottom, followed by the chicken. Sprinkle with cinnamon, salt and pepper, then top with the tomatoes. Cover and cook on low heat for 8 - 9 hours, or until vegetables and chicken are tender.

Transfer chicken to a bowl, then cover to keep warm.

Add lemon peel, tomato paste, and oregano to the sauce in the slow cooker. Mix to combine. Allow the sauce to thicken for about 15 minutes.

Meanwhile, debone the chicken, break into large pieces. Add to the slow cooker. Spoon stew into shallow bowls and serve with parsley on top.

Enjoy!

4. Greek Beefy Pita Sandwich

Bursting with veggies and ground beef, these Pita folds make a fabulous Greek meal ready in just 20 minutes.

4 soft Greek **pita breads** (heated)
1 lb. (450 g) **lean beef** (ground)
¼ cup **olives** (sliced)
½ cup **cucumber** (peeled, chopped)
½ cup **tomato** (seeded, chopped)
1 tsp **dill weed** (dried)
1 small **onion** (halved lengthwise, sliced)
3 cloves **garlic** (finely chopped)
1 tsp **oregano** leaves (dried)
1 cup **Greek yogurt**
½ tsp **salt**

Makes 4 servings
Calories: 390 per serving

Heat a large pan over medium-high heat. Add beef, oregano, garlic, onion, and half the salt to the pan and cook for 5-6 minutes, while stirring. Remove from heat and add olives.

In a medium bowl, mix yogurt, cucumber, tomato, dill and the remaining half of salt.

Scoop one quarter of the beef mixture on one half of the pita bread and top each with yogurt mixture. Fold other half of the pita bread over filling.

Serve with remaining yogurt mixture on the side.

Enjoy!

5. Pepper and Pork

This is a delightfully simple but delicious slow-cooker recipe that can be served in numerous ways.

2 lbs. (900 g) **pork tenderloin** (fat trimmed)
2 tbs **Greek seasoning** (or more to taste)
1 lb. (450 g) jar **peperoncini peppers** (with juice)

Makes 8 servings
Calories: 105 per serving

Place all ingredients in a slow cooker and cook on high heat for about 4 hours.

Shred pork into small pieces and cook for about 12 more minutes.

Either serve with chips and dip, as filling for a taco roll, or as filling for a submarine sandwich.

Enjoy!

6. Greek Chicken Salad

Chicken, feta cheese and chickpeas are all protein-rich that will surely fill an empty stomach. Ready in 10 minutes, not to include preparation of roasted chicken.

2 whole-**wheat pitas**
½ cup red **onion** (thinly sliced)
1 ½ cups **cherry tomatoes**
10 oz. (280 g) **chickpeas** (drained, rinsed)
8 cups **romaine lettuce** (shredded)
½ cup **radish** (sliced)
1 green **bell pepper** (cored, seeded, cut into strips)
1/3 cup **feta** (crumbled)
¼ cup fresh **dill** (chopped)
½ **cucumber** (peeled, sliced)
2 cups roasted **chicken** (skinless)
¼ cup **kalamata olives** (chopped, pitted)
1 tbs extra-virgin **olive oil**
2 tbs fresh **lemon juice**

Makes 4 servings
Calories: 375 per serving

Preheat oven to 200°F (95°C).

Wrap pitas in tin foil and place in the oven.

In a bowl, combine all of the ingredients except for the oil and lemon juice.

In another bowl, mix lemon juice and oil, then sprinkle over salad. Toss to coat.

Remove pitas from oven and cut into quarters.

Divide the ingredient mix into 4 equal portions and serve with 2 pita quarters each.

Enjoy!

7. Greek Pita Lunch

This 30 minute Pita lunch uses Tahini dressing, but you can also use your favorite dressing instead.

2 whole **pita breads** (halved)
1 lb. (450 g) **cottage cheese** (whisked)
1 tsp **oregano** (dried)
½ cup **mixed sprouts**
3 cloves **garlic** (finely minced)
1 cup **feta cheese** (crumbled)
1 tsp **basil** (dried)
2 medium **tomatoes** (chopped)
1 tbs **tahini**
1 red **onion** (cut in rings)
12 **spinach** leaves (washed and dried)
1 medium sweet **green pepper** (chopped)
Pepper

Dressing:
1 cup **tahini**
1 tsp **cumin**
¼ cup **parsley** (minced)
1 **lemon** (juiced)
1 dash **cayenne**
3/4 cup **water**
2 tsp **tamari**

Makes 4 servings
Calories: 375 per serving

Preheat oven to 400°F (200°C). In a bowl, mix cottage cheese with oregano, garlic, tahini, feta and basil. Sprinkle pepper to taste.

Scoop about ½ cup of the cheese mixture into each half pita pocket and bake for about 6 minutes. Add onion rings, pepper, spinach, tomatoes and sprouts to each pita pocket.

Meanwhile, mix tahini with lemon juice. Stir in water until dissolved. Mix in tamari cayenne, cumin, and parsley.

Serve pita with tahini dressing and enjoy!

8. Turkey Sausage Meal

This Mediterranean one-dish meal is packed with vegetables, Greek olives and feta cheese. It takes 25 minutes to prepare.

¾ lb. (340 g) **Italian turkey sausage** (chopped)
14 oz. (400 g) **tomatoes** (unsalted, diced)
½ cup **feta cheese** (crumbled)
¼ cup **Greek olives**
1 tsp **oregano** (dried)
½ cup **quinoa** (rinsed)
3 cups **baby spinach**
1 medium **onion** (chopped)
2 cloves **garlic** (minced)

Makes 4 servings
Calories: 285 per serving

In a lightly greased non-stick pan, cook onion and sausage over medium heat until softened and browned. Stir in garlic and cook for another minute. Add oregano, tomatoes, and olives, then bring to boil.

Add quinoa and stir to combine. Place spinach on top, lower heat, cover and bring to a simmer for about 12 minutes. Remove from heat.

Gently stir mixture to loosen up. Sprinkle cheese on top.

Enjoy!

9. Greek-Flavoured Shrimp

This dish is strongly spiced with allspice and cinnamon. It takes 1 hour to prepare.

1 ¼ lb. (550 g) large **shrimp** (peeled)
2/3 cup **feta** (crumbled)
1 medium **onion** (chopped)
½ tsp **red-pepper** flakes
½ tsp **cinnamon** (ground)
2 garlic **cloves** (chopped)
3 tbs extra-virgin **olive oil**
1/4 tsp ground **allspice**
28 oz. (800 g) canned **tomatoes** (diced)
2 tbs **dill** (chopped)
1/8 tsp **salt**

Makes 4 servings
Calories: 345 per serving

Preheat oven to 375°F (190°C). Place rack in the middle of the oven.

In a skillet, heat oil over medium heat and sauté garlic and onion for about 5 minutes, or until tender.

Add salt and spices, then cook for about 30 seconds while stirring. Add tomatoes and its juice. Let it simmer for about 20 minutes, or until just thickened, stirring once or twice. Remove from heat.

Add salt to the shrimp and stir into tomato sauce. Spread mixture on a baking dish, top with feta and bake for about 20 minutes, or until cooked. Sprinkle with dill and serve.

Enjoy!

10. Turkey Salad Wraps

30 minutes is all that is needed to have a healthy, fresh and crunchy lunch that can be packed and enjoyed outdoors.

12 oz. (340 g) **turkey breast** (cooked, shredded)
12 heads **lettuce leaves**
1 cup green **apple** (chopped)
6 oz. (170 g) **Greek plain yogurt**
¼ cup **walnuts** (chopped, toasted)
¼ cup **tart cherries**
½ cup green **onions** (sliced)
½ cup **celery** (chopped)
½ hot **pepper sauce**
½ cup **flat-leaf parsley** (chopped)
2 tbs **lemon juice**
¼ tsp each **salt** and ground **black pepper**

Makes 4 servings
Calories: 225 per serving

In a bowl, mix turkey with green onions, parsley, celery, walnuts, apple, and dried cherries. Set aside.

In a separate bowl, mix yogurt with hot pepper sauce, lemon juice, salt and black pepper. Mix well to blend.

Spoon turkey mixture on the center of lettuce leaves and top with yogurt mixture. Roll the leaves into wraps.

Alternatively, use spinach leaves instead of lettuce leaves and wrap everything into a whole-wheat tortilla.

Enjoy!

Section 3: Dinner

1. Greek Lentils with Pita Wedges

Delicious slow-cooked lentils served with pita wedges. This meals is cooked in 4 hours.

4 pita breads
2 ½ oz. (70 g) **olives** (drained, sliced)
20 oz. (550 g) condensed **chicken broth**
2 tsp **lemon peel** (grated)
¼ cup **feta cheese** (crumbled)
2 cups **lentils** (sorted, rinsed)
2 medium **green onions** (sliced)
1 large **onion** (chopped)
4 cups **water**
1 cup sun-dried **tomatoes** (chopped)

Makes 6 servings
Calories: 367 per serving

In a lightly greased slow cooker, combine onion, olives, chicken broth, lentils and water. Cover and cook on high heat for 3-4 hours.

Meanwhile, in a bowl, soak tomatoes in warm water. Set aside.

An hour before the slow cooker is done, add soaked tomatoes and lemon peel to the slow cooker. Stir to combine.

Transfer to serving bowls, topped with onions and cheese. Cut pita breads into 6 wedges. Serve 1 wedge with each serving.

Enjoy!

2. Greek Roasted Chicken

This meal is great to be served to family members. 2 hours is all it takes to prepare this sumptuous dinner.

7 lbs. (3 kg) roasted **chicken**
¾ cup **chicken broth**
5 baking **potatoes** (peeled, quartered)
¼ cup **butter** (melted)
2 ½ tsp dried **oregano** (divided)
3 tbs **lemon juice**
Salt and **pepper** to taste

Makes 9 servings
Calories; 215 per serving

Preheat oven to 350°F (180°C).

In a roasting pan, combine chicken with salt and pepper. Slowly sprinkle half of the oregano until well distributed.

Arrange chicken breast side up, and potatoes on their sides. Sprinkle more oregano and salt and pepper to taste. Drizzle lemon juice and melted butter, then add the broth.

Bake for about 75 minutes, brushing regularly with pan drippings, until temperature inside meat reaches 180°F (80°C).

Remove and allow to cool under a loose tin foil. Transfer drippings to a pan and heat until thickened. Glaze sauce over chicken slices.

Enjoy!

3. Greek Chicken Dinner

This chicken dinner is ready after 1 hour of preparation and cooking.

1 lbs. (450 g) **chicken** (cut up)
2 medium **carrots** (sliced)
1 medium **potato** (cubed)
3 tbs **olive oil**
1 small **onion** (quartered)
1 tsp **basil** (dried)
1 tsp **parsley** (minced)
2 tbs **lemon juice**
1/8 tsp **garlic** powder
¼ tsp **oregano** (dried)
Salt and **pepper** to taste

Makes 2 servings
Calories: 305 per serving

Preheat oven to 360°F (180°C). Lightly grease a baking dish.

In a large pan, heat 1 tablespoon oil and cook chicken until browned on all sides.

In the prepared baking dish, combine potato, carrots and onion. Add remaining oil, then toss to coat. Place chicken on top.

In a small bowl, combine garlic powder, parsley, oregano, basil, salt and pepper. Sprinkle mixture over chicken and vegetables, then drizzle with lemon juice.

Cover and bake for about 45 minutes. Remove cover and bake for another 15 minutes, or until chicken juices ooze out and vegetables are softened.

Enjoy!

4. Greek Broiled Tilapia Fillets

These tilapia fillets are broiled and topped with a mixture of onion, dill, olives and feta cheese for a tangy Greek-inspired flavour. The cooking time is 25 minutes.

8 times 4 oz. (110g) **tilapia fillets**
½ cup **feta cheese** (crumbled)
¼ cup **Greek plain yogurt**
1 small **red onion** (chopped)
½ cup **Greek olives** (pitted)
2 tbs **butter** or **coconut butter** (softened)
1 tbs **lime juice**
¼ tsp **garlic** powder
1 tsp **dill weed**
½ tsp **paprika**
¼ tsp each **salt** and **pepper**

Makes 8 servings
Calories: 155 per serving

Preheat a broiler.

Rub tilapia with salt and pepper. Place on a lightly greased broiler pan.

In a bowl, mix yogurt with lime juice and the butter of your choice. Stir in olives, onion, and seasonings. Coat each fillet and drizzle with feta cheese.

Broil for about 8 minutes, or until fork tender.

Enjoy!

5. Lamb Kebabs

Kebabs are always a win on parties as well as the dinner table. Preparation starts in the morning, if the kebabs are supposed to be served in the evening.

1 lb. (450 g) boneless **lamb** (cubed)
16 **cherry tomatoes**
4 tsp **olive oil**
½ cup **lemon juice**
2 tbs **oregano** (dried)
1 large **green pepper** (sliced)
1 large **onion** (chopped)
6 cloves **garlic** (minced)
8 metal or wooden **skewers**

Makes 4 servings
Calories: 207 per serving

In a small bowl, combine lemon juice and oil with oregano and garlic. Chill ¼ cup for later.

In a sealable plastic container, combine remaining marinade with lamb. Mix, cover and chill for at least 8 hours or overnight. Optionally, mix once or twice during the marinating process.

Remove lamb from the plastic container, discarding the marinade.

For the kebabs, place lamb, tomatoes, green pepper and onion on the skewers in alternating order.

Heat a griller and moisten it with oil.

Grill kebabs over medium heat for about 6 minutes on each side, or until lamb is cooked and vegetables are tender. Baste with reserved ¼ cup marinade and turn kebabs occasionally as they grill.

Serve 2 skewers per serving.

Enjoy!

6. Greek Feta Casserole

Feta cheese and cinnamon provides a distinct Greek taste for this hot dish, prepared in just an hour.

½ cup **elbow macaroni**
2 tbs **milk**
1 whole **egg** (lightly beaten)
¼ tsp ground **cinnamon**
½ cup **feta cheese** (crumbled, divided)
2 tbs **onion** (chopped)
½ cup **tomato sauce**
½ lb. (225 g) ground **pork**

Makes 2 servings
Calories: 396 per serving

Cook macaroni al dente according to package instructions.

Preheat oven to 375°F (190°C).

In a bowl, whisk egg with ¼ cup cheese and milk. Add cooked macaroni, stir and transfer to a greased baking dish.

Heat a skillet over medium heat. Add pork and onion and cook until meat is browned and onion softened. Drain excess fat, then stir in cinnamon and tomato sauce.

Pour pork mixture over macaroni, sprinkle with remaining cheese, cover and bake for about 20 minutes. Remove cover and bake for another 15 minutes, or until bubbles begin to form.

Enjoy!

7. Greek Beef Stew

A slow cooked beef stew that is served over orzo pasta. The cooking time is about 10 hours.

3 cups cooked **orzo pasta**
2 lbs. (900 g) lean **beef round roas**t (trimmed, cubed)
¾ tsp ground **cinnamon**
2 cups small **onions**
1/3 cup **all-purpose flour**
¾ cup **tomato paste**
¾ cup dry **red wine** (or apple juice)
1 tbs **red wine vinegar**
1 ½ cups **water**
1 tbs **honey**
½ cup **feta cheese** (crumbled, optional)

Makes 6 servings
Calories: 315 per serving

In a bowl, combine beef with cinnamon and flour. Transfer to a slow cooker. Add onions, water, wine, vinegar, tomato paste, and honey. Mix to blend.

Cover and cook on low heat for about 10 hours, or until beef is tender. Serve over pasta with cheese on top.

Enjoy!

8. Greek Egg Frittata

A lovely egg frittata that's ready in 30 minutes.

8 whole **eggs**
1 tbs **vegetable oil**
½ cup **milk**
¼ tsp **salt**
¼ tsp **pepper**
1 ½ cups **spinach** (bite-size pieces)
½ cup **feta cheese** (crumbled)
1 tbs fresh **oregano leaves** (chopped)
2/3 cup **potatoes**
1/3 cup **onions** and **peppers** (mixed)

Makes 4 servings
Calories: 274 per serving

In a bowl, whisk eggs with milk, salt and pepper until smooth. Stir in feta cheese and set aside.

Heat oil in a pan over medium heat. Add potatoes and oregano, then cook for 3-4 minutes. Add spinach and stir-cook for about 1 minute, or until potatoes are tender.

Lower heat to medium-low and pour in the egg mixture. Cover and cook for about 8 minutes, or until bottom turns light brown.

Place frittata in the oven and broil for 2-3 minutes, or until top begins to turn brown.

Enjoy!

9. Spicy Chicken Burgers

A Burger with chicken, yogurt, edamame and avocado - a tasty and nutritious combination.

2 skinless **chicken breasts** (quartered)
¼ cup plain **Greek yogurt**
1 tsp **white wine** vinegar
½ tsp **sugar**
½ small **red onion** (diced, divided)
1 ripe **avocado** (diced)
1 cup **cucumber** (thinly sliced)
1 tbs **olive oil**
1 cup frozen **edamame** (thawed, shelled)
1 **Portobello** cap
2 tbs low-sodium **soy sauce**
2 cloves **garlic**
¼ tsp **cayenne pepper**
4 whole grain **buns** (split)
Lettuce leaves (optional)

Makes 4 servings
Calories: 357 per serving

Preheat oven to 400°F (200°C).

In a bowl, mix yogurt with sugar and vinegar. Add avocado, cucumber and half the onions. Gently mix to coat. Set aside.

In a food processor, combine edamame, garlic, Portobello, and remaining half of onion, then process until finely chopped. Add chicken, cayenne, and soy sauce. Pulse several times until well incorporated. Form mixture into 4 patties.

In a heat-proof pan, heat oil over high heat. Cook patties for about 3 minutes per side, or until both sides are browned. Transfer pan to the oven and bake for about 15 minutes, or until patties are well cooked through.

Place patties on bottom halves of muffins, put lettuce and top each with ½ cup avocado mixture. Sandwich them with top muffin halves.

10. Greek Spiced Squid

An exotic Mediterranean dish, this squid is marinated with different herbs, enriching its tangy taste.

1 lb. (450 g) cleaned **squid** (cut into rings)
5 tbs **olive oil**
1 ½ cups **water**
1 **onion** (sliced)
¼ cup fresh **parsley** (minced)
2 cloves **garlic** (peeled)
8 whole black **peppercorns**
2 large **rosemary** sprigs
½ cup **white wine vinegar**
1 **bay leaf**
12 **baguette bread** slices

Makes 6 servings
Calories: 340 per serving

In a large pan, heat 1 ½ cups water and 3 tbs oil over medium heat. Add the squid and onion, cover and simmer 15 minutes.

Add rosemary and parsley, cover and continue cooking for about 10 minutes, or until squid is tender.

Transfer mixture to large container with lid. Add garlic, vinegar, bay leaf and peppercorns. Tightly seal and chill overnight up to 3 days.

Meanwhile, preheat broiler. Baste baguette slices with 2 tbs oil and broil until golden. Set aside.

Drain squid mixture, discarding all other herbs and spices. Transfer squid mixture to a serving bowl, season with salt and pepper, and drizzle with additional olive oil.

Serve with toasted baguette slices.

Enjoy!

Section 4: Side Dishes

1. Greek Lemony Rice

A Greek rice treat that is ready in 25 minutes.

½ cup long grain **rice**
1 tsp **chicken bouillon** granules
1 tsp fresh **mint** (minced)
1/8 tsp **garlic** powder
1 cup **water**
1 ½ tsp **butter**
1 tsp **lemon juice**

Makes 2 servings
Calories: 175 per serving

In a small pot, combine rice with the rest of the ingredients and boil over medium-high heat.

Turn heat to low, cover and simmer for 15 minutes, or until tender and water is well absorbed.

Enjoy!

2. Green Beans with Tomatoes

Green beans cooked with a Mediterranean touch. It is done in 20 minutes.

2 cups fresh **green beans** (cut)
1 small **tomato** (chopped)
½ small **sweet onion** (sliced)
½ tsp **oregano** (dried)
1 tbs **olive oil**
¼ tsp **salt**
1 dash **pepper**

Makes 2 servings
Calories: 95 per serving

In a pot, cover beans with water and boil over medium heat for about 4 minutes, or until beans are tender and crisp. Remove the water.

In a small pan, heat oil and cook onions for about 3 minutes, or until tender. Add the beans and cook for about 5 minutes. Lower heat, add the rest of the ingredients and cook for 1 more minute.

Enjoy!

3. Greek Tomatoes with Onions

Tomatoes, more especially if home-grown, are great with grilled meat and roasted corn.

¾ cup **feta cheese** (crumbled)
4 medium **tomatoes** (sliced)
1 tbs **olive oil**
¼ cup fresh **parsley** (minced)
1 small **red onion** (cut into rings)
½ tsp each **salt** and **pepper**

Makes 6 servings
Calories: 97 per serving

On a plate, arrange onion slices alternately with tomato slices.

Sprinkle with cheese and parsley, season with salt and pepper, and drizzle with oil.

Cover and chill for at least 15 minutes.

Enjoy!

4. Pasta with Olives and Romano Cheese

A vegetarian pasta side dish with basil, olives, tomatoes and olive oil. It is ready in less than 30 minutes.

16 oz. (450 g) **spiral pasta**
6 oz. (170 g) **Greek olives** (pitted, drained)
½ cup **Romano cheese** (grated)
¼ cup **olive oil**
¾ cup sun-dried **tomatoes** (oil-packed)
1 tsp **lime** juice
1 tbs **capers** (drained)
¼ tsp **red pepper** flakes (crushed)
¼ tsp **pepper**
¾ cup fresh **basil** (minced)

Makes 10 servings
Calories: 197 per serving

Cook the pasta al dente according to package instructions. Drain into a colander and rinse with cold water.

In a large bowl, combine the rest of the ingredients, except basil. Mix to blend. Set aside for about 15 minutes for flavour to develop.

Combine pasta with the mixture and basil leaves. Toss to coat.

Enjoy!

5. Baked Pasta with Greek Cheeses

Orzo pasta is delightfully baked with 2 Greek cheeses. A very delicious side dish ready in 45 minutes.

1 lb. (450 g) **orzo pasta**
14 oz. (400 g) **chicken broth**
½ lb. (225 g) **feta cheese** (crumbled)
½ cup **whipping cream**
¼ cup **olive oil**
1 tbs **dill** (chopped)
1/3 cup **Kasseri cheese** (grated)
Salt and **Pepper** (to taste)

Makes 8 servings
Calories: 357 per serving

Fill a large pot with broth and water. Add salt and boil over high heat. Add orzo and cook until al dente, stirring occasionally.

Drain in a colander, rinse with cold water and transfer to a baking dish. Add the rest of the ingredients. Cling wrap and let chill overnight.

Preheat oven to 350°F (180°C).

Drizzle with feta cheese and bake for about 40 minutes.

Enjoy!

6. Greek Sautéed Vegetables

Mushrooms are astoundingly healthy foods and go great with zucchini and potatoes. This tasteful side dish is ready in 45 minutes.

1 large **zucchini** (chopped)
10 crimini **mushrooms** (quartered)
8 red **potatoes** (quartered)
1 tsp **oregano** (dried)
6 tbs **olive oil**
1 clove **garlic** (minced)
Salt and **pepper** (to taste)

Makes 6 servings
Calories: 125 per serving

In a pan, heat oil over medium heat. Place oregano and garlic, then sauté for about 1 minute. Season with salt and pepper to taste.

Add zucchini, potatoes, and mushrooms. Cover and cook over high heat for about 15 minutes.

Lower heat and stir. Cover again and continue cooking for about 5 more minutes, or until vegetables are tender.

Enjoy!

7. Green Garden Fries

Oven fried vegetables served with a lemony Greek yogurt dip. This side dish is prepared within 40 minutes.

Fries
2 **eggs** (beaten)
¼ tsp **salt**
2 tbs **butter** (melted)
3 tbs all-purpose **flour**
1 cup **panko bread** crumbs
1 ½ lbs. (680 g) **broccolini** or **zucchini**
½ cup **parmesan cheese** (finely shredded)
1 tbs **basil, dill, oregano,** or **thyme**

Dip
6 oz. (170 g) plain **Greek yogurt**
1 clove **garlic** (chopped)
1 tbs **olive oil**
½ tsp **salt**
1 tbs **lemon** juice
2 tbs **basil, dill, oregano,** or **thyme**

Makes 6 servings
Calories: 249 per serving

Combine all dip-ingredients in a small bowl. Cover and chill. Preheat oven to 400°F (200°C). Lightly grease a cookie sheet and line it with tin foil.

Get 3 shallow bowls. Put flour into one bowl, eggs into the second, and a mixture of bread crumbs, cheese, 1 tbs herbs and salt into the third. For the herbs, choose either basil, dill, oregano, or thyme.

Dip and roll vegetables in the flour, dip into eggs, then coat with the mixture.
Arrange coated vegetables on the prepared cookie sheet. Drizzle melted butter on the vegetables and bake for about 20 minutes, or until golden brown.

Serve with the dip and enjoy!

8. Greek Marinated Pasta

A marinated pasta with vegetables and salami. This side dish is ready in less than 3 hours.

1 lb. (450 g) **orecchiette pasta**
7 oz. (200 g) **red bell peppers** (chopped)
6 **pepperoncini pepper** (halved)
¼ lb. (115 g) **deli olive** (pitted, halved)
½ lb. (225 g) hard **salami** (cut into strips)
1 ½ cups **Greek dressing** with **feta**
2 cups **grape tomatoes** (halved)
¼ cup **Italian parsley leaves** (chopped)
½ English **cucumber** (thinly sliced)
1 cup **feta cheese** (crumbled)

Makes 16 servings
Calories: 248 per serving

Cook pasta according to package instructions. Drain and rinse with cold water.

In a large bowl, combine cooked pasta with olives, salami, pepperoncini peppers, roasted peppers, and cucumber. Stir in 1 cup of the dressing, then toss to coat. Cling wrap and chill for at least 2 hours or overnight.

Just before serving, stir in parsley, tomatoes and remaining ½ cup dressing. Drizzle cheese.

Enjoy!

9. Couscous with Carrot and Zucchini

This side dish combines colorful vegetables with couscous. It is ready within 15 minutes.

½ cup **couscous** (uncooked)
½ cup **zucchini** (chopped)
½ cup **carrot** (chopped)
¾ cup **water**
1 tbs **butter**
1 **green onion** (thinly sliced)
½ cup **onion** (chopped)
½ tsp **salt**
1/8 tsp **white pepper**

Makes 2 servings
Calories: 215 per serving

Bring water to a boil in a saucepan. Add couscous, cover and remove from heat. Let soak for about 5 minutes.

In a pan, heat butter and cook onion and carrot for about 4 minutes, or until tender and crisp.

Add green onion and zucchini, then cook for 3 more minutes, or until tender. Season with salt and pepper.

With a fork or spatula, loosen up couscous, add sautéed vegetable and mix to blend.

Enjoy!

10. Greek Potatoes with Oregano

These baked potato cubes are spiced with oregano and are very easy to prepare. This side dish is ready in less than 1 hour.

2 medium **potatoes** (peeled, cubed)
1 garlic **clove** (minced)
1 ½ tsp fresh **oregano** (minced)
5 tsp **olive oil**
2 tbs **lemon juice**
½ tsp **salt**
1/8 tsp **pepper**

Makes 2 servings
Calories: 216 per serving

Preheat oven to 425°F (220°C).

In a lightly greased baking dish, combine all of the ingredients. Mix to blend.

Transfer to oven and bake for about 45-50 minutes, or until potatoes are tender.

Enjoy!

Section 5: Snacks

1. Cheesy Cracker Bread with Olives

A quick and simple Greek snack ready in 15 minutes.

1/3 cup **kalamata olives** (pitted, halved)
1 **cracker bread**
1 tbs fresh **basil leaves** (chopped)
1 ½ cups **Italian cheese** (shredded)

Makes 15 servings
Calories: 87 per serving

Preheat oven to 380°F (190°C).

Place bread on a baking sheet. Distribute olives and cheese and bake for about 5 minutes, or until cheese melts.

Slice cracker bread into desired serving sizes.

Serve warm.

Enjoy!

2. Banana Strawberry Smoothie

A fruity Greek yogurt smoothie that is ready in 5 minutes.

1 medium **banana** (sliced)
1 cup fresh **strawberries**
1 ½ cups **skim milk**
6 oz. (170 g) **Greek strawberry yogurt**

Makes 2 servings
Calories: 195 per serving

Combine all ingredients in a food processor and blend until smooth. Serve in tall glasses. Garnish with fresh strawberries.

Enjoy!

3. Greek Nachos with Hummus

Tacos with hummus and feta cheese that are topped with kalamata olives. This is a fabulous Greek snack and ready in 15 minutes.

1 **tortilla** (taco sized, cut into 4 wedges)
2 tbs **feta cheese**
8 **kalamata olives** (halved)
2 tbs **hummus**
2 tbs **red onion** (minced)
¼ cup **tomato** (chopped)
Fresh **parsley** (chopped)
2 tsp **Greek vinaigrette**

Makes 4 wedges
Calories: 195 per wedge

Preheat oven to 400°F (200°C).

Place tortilla wedges on a lightly greased baking sheet and bake for about 4 minutes, or until lightly browned.

On each of the toasted wedge, put about ½ tsp hummus and about ½ tsp feta cheese. Top with 2 olives, ½ tbs red onion, tomato, and ½ tsp Greek vinaigrette.

Return to oven and bake for about 4-5 minutes, or until golden brown. Garnish with chopped fresh parsley.

Enjoy!

4. Layered Greek Dip

Hummus, tomato, cucumber, feta cheese and green onions are layered to form this delicious Greek Dip. Ready in 30 minutes.

8 oz. (225 g) **cream cheese** (softened)
3 cloves **garlic** (pressed)
1 tbs **lemon juice**
1 tsp **Italian seasoning** (dried)
1 cup **cucumber** (chopped)
1 cup **tomatoes** (chopped)
1 cup **hummus** (prepared)
1/3 cup **green onions** (sliced)
1/2 cup **feta cheese** (crumbled)
Pita chips (multigrain, for dipping)

Makes 2 servings
Calories: 170 per serving

Into a mixing bowl whisked cream cheese with lemon juice, garlic and Italian seasoning until smooth.

On a 9 inch serving dish, layer the cream cheese mixture, followed by a spread of hummus. Top with tomato, cucumber, feta cheese and green onions. Cling wrap and chill overnight.

Enjoy with pita chips.

5. Greek Cheese Puffs

In this recipe, eggs and cheese are filo wrapped to form puffs. They are ready in an hour.

1 lb. (450 g) **phyllo pastry** (frozen, thawed)
3 oz. (85 g) **cream cheese** (softened)
2 whole **eggs**
4 oz. (115 g) **feta cheese**
¼ cup **cottage cheese**
Unsalted **butter** (melted)

Makes 4 servings
Calories: 296 per serving

Preheat oven to 375°F (190°C).

In a bowl, whisk eggs using a hand mixer until smooth. Add cheese and mix again. Set aside.

On a wax paper covered surface, unfold a phyllo sheet and cut lengthwise into 3 strips. Brush top sides with butter, fold in half and brush top sides again.

Put 1 tsp of the egg-cheese mixture at base of each strip. Lift one bottom corner and fold over the cheese mixture, forming a triangle. Continue the folding pattern, pressing corners together to seal them.

Transfer triangles to an ungreased cookie sheet and brush with butter.

Repeat the process with the remaining phyllo sheets.

Bake for about 15 minutes, or until golden.

Enjoy!

6. Cheesy au Gratin Potato Cupcakes

Although designed to be a side dish during lunch and breakfast, these cupcakes are perfect snacks. They are ready in less than an hour.

6 oz. (175 g) **au gratin potatoes**
¼ cup **salsa**
2 **eggs** (beaten)
6 oz. (170 g) **Greek yogurt**
Green onions (sliced, optional)

Makes 6 servings
Calories: 153 per serving

Preheat oven to 375°F (190°C). Lightly grease 12 muffin cups.

Prepare au gratin potatoes according to package instructions. Omit butter and milk. Mix in eggs and salsa.

Fill each muffin cup with batter, about 1/3 of a cup. Transfer to oven and bake for about 30 minutes, or until tops are golden brown.

Allow to cool for about 5 minutes, then remove the cupcakes from the muffin cups.

Top each cupcake with ½ oz. yoghurt and optionally garnish with onions.

Enjoy!

7. Greek Pretzel Nuggets

These pretzel nuggets with herbs and seasonings are a winner on parties and movie nights. They are prepared in 30 minutes.

2 packs of 1 lb. (450 g) **pretzel nuggets**
1 **salad dressing** mix
¼ cup **olive oil**
½ tsp **garlic powder**
½ tsp **onion powder**
1 tsp **dill weed**
1 ½ tsp **oregano** (dried)
1 tsp **lemon-pepper seasoning**

Makes 18 servings
Calories: 155 per serving

Preheat oven to 350°F (180°C). Lightly grease a baking pan.

In a bowl, combine the dressing mix with the rest of the ingredients. Add the pretzels last, then toss to coat.

Spread nuggets on prepared baking pan and bake for about 10 minutes. Move pretzels a bit, then bake for another 5 minutes. Allow to cool.

Enjoy!

8. Greek Dip with Pita Chips

This recipe gives pits chips a Mediterranean flair. They are ready in 30 minutes.

6 **pita breads** (cut into wedges)
1 and ¾ tsp **garlic powder** (divided)
12 oz. (340 g) **cream cheese**
1 cup **Greek plain yogurt**
1 tsp **oregano** (dried)
¾ tsp **coriander** (ground)
¼ tsp **pepper**
1 large **tomato** (chopped)
5 **pepperoncini** (sliced)
½ cup **Greek olives** (pitted, sliced)
1 medium **cucumber** (diced)
1/3 cup **feta cheese** (crumbled)
2 tbs **parsley** (minced)

Makes 18 servings
Calories: 169 per serving

Preheat oven to 350°F (180°C).

Place chip wedges on an ungreased baking sheet. Brush all sides with butter and sprinkle with 1 tsp garlic powder. Bake for about 6 minutes on each side, or until golden brown. Cool on wire racks.

For the dip, in a bowl, whisk yogurt with cream cheese, coriander, oregano, pepper and remaining garlic powder.

Pour dip into a pie plate. Top with tomato, pepperoncini, olives, cucumber, feta cheese and parsley. Serve with the pita chips.

Enjoy!

9. Beans with Roasted Sweet Pepper

A delicious bean and pepper recipes that has more to give than it seems at first. It is prepared in 30 minutes.

30 oz. (850 g) **garbanzo beans**
2 large sweet **red pepper**
1/3 cup **lemon juice**
½ tsp **coriander** (ground)
½ tsp **cumin** (ground)
3 tbs **tahini**
1 tbs **olive oil**
2 garlic **cloves** (peeled)
1 tsp **curry powder**
½ tsp **pepper**
1 ¼ tsp **salt**
Pita bread (warmed, cut into wedges)
Wheat snack crackers

Makes 12 servings
Calories: 125 per serving

Broil red peppers for about 5 minutes, rotating every minute. At this point, their skins should be blistered and slightly blackened.

Allow to cool for 15-20 minutes. Remove charred skin, stem and seeds.

Place broiled peppers, beans, tahini, lemon juice, garlic, oil, and seasonings in in a food processor. Process until pureed.

Serve in a bowl with crackers and pita bread. Garnish with more beans.

Enjoy!

10. Greek Spiced Walnut Cake

A walnut-based cake with Mediterranean-inspired glaze. It takes 45 minutes to bake this nutty treat.

Cake
1 ½ cups **whole-wheat flour**
½ cup **barley flour**
1 ¼ cups **walnuts** (chopped, divided)
2 tsp **baking powder**
¾ tsp **cloves** (ground)
½ tsp **baking soda**
2 whole **eggs**
1 tsp **cinnamon** (ground)
¼ tsp **nutmeg** (ground)
¼ tsp **salt**
½ cup **orange juice**
¼ cup **olive oil**
¾ cup light **brown sugar**
2/3 cup **Greek yogurt**
2 tsp fresh **orange zest**

Syrup
1 small strip **orange zest**
2 whole **cloves**
1/3 cup **orange juice**
¼ cup light **brown sugar**

Makes 12 servings
Calories: 275 per serving

Preheat oven to 350°F (180°C). Lightly grease and flour-dust a glass baking dish.

Roast walnuts in oven for about 7 minutes, or until aromatic. Remove and allow to cool on a plate. Lower oven temperature to 300°F (150°C).

In a large bowl, combine flour with baking soda, baking powder, nutmeg, cinnamon, cloves, and salt. Mix until well incorporated.

In a small bowl, mix yogurt with orange juice and zest.

In another bowl, whip eggs with sugar until smooth. Slowly mix in yogurt mixture and oil.

Gradually pour wet mixture into the flour mixture, stirring until a batter is formed. Add walnuts and fold to combine.

Transfer to prepared dish and bake for about 40 minutes, or until toothpick comes out clean when inserted. Allow to cool on a wire rack.

Meanwhile, in a saucepan, combine orange juice, orange zest strip, brown sugar, and cloves. Boil over medium-high heat while stirring. Lower heat and simmer for about 5 minutes, or until thickened. Discard cloves and the zest. Set aside to cool.

Glaze syrup all over the cake. Repeat glazing until well seeped in. Drizzle the remaining walnuts on top. Remove cake from dish and cut to desired slices.

Enjoy!

Printed in Great Britain
by Amazon